Taking Cancer to School

D0730981

WITHDRAWN

APR 1 8 2020

UNBC Library

UNIVERSITY of NORTHERN
BRITISH COLUMBIA
LIBRARY
Prince George, B.C.

by Cynthia S. Henry and Kim Gosselin

Adapted for the Special Kids in School® series

JayJo Books, L.L.C.

Publishing Special Books for Special Kids®

Taking Cancer to School
© 2001 Kim Gosselin
Edited by Karen Schader

All rights reserved. No part of this book may be reproduced or transmitted in any form or by any means, electronic or mechanical, including photocopying, recording, or by any information storage and retrieval system without written permission from the publisher. Printed in the United States of America.

Published by
JayJo Books, LLC
A Guidance Channel Company
Publishing Special Books for Special Kids®

JayJo Books is a publisher of books to help teachers, parents, and children cope with chronic illnesses, special needs, and health education in classroom, family, and social settings.

Library of Congress Control Number: 2001087646
ISBN 1-891383-11-6
First Edition
Eighth book in our *Special Kids in School*® series

For information about
Premium and Special Sales, contact:
JayJo Books Special Sales Office
P.O. Box 213
Valley Park, MO 63088-0213
636-861-1331
jayjobooks@aol.com
www.jayjo.com

For all other information, contact:
JayJo Books
A Guidance Channel Company
135 Dupont Street, P.O. Box 760
Plainview, NY 11803-0760
1-800-999-6884
jayjobooks@guidancechannel.com
www.jayjo.com

The opinions in this book are solely those of the author. Medical care is highly individualized and should never be altered without professional medical consultation.

Dedication

*To the courageous children and families living with cancer
and the dedicated doctors and nurses
who treat them*

About the Authors

*Cynthia Snavely Henry lives in Lititz, Pennsylvania with her husband Corky,
and two children, Alexandra and Chase. Her interest in children's health issues began
when her son was diagnosed with a potentially fatal food allergy. She is the author of
Taking Cystic Fibrosis to School and is committed to bringing awareness to children's
health issues. She is an active community leader in school, childcare, nonprofit, and sports
organizations.*

*Kim Gosselin began her writing career with a heartfelt desire and determination to
educate the classmates of children with special needs and/or chronic conditions. An avid
supporter of the American Lung Association, American Cancer Society, the Epilepsy
Foundation of America, American Diabetes Association, Juvenile Diabetes Research
Foundation, and CHADD, Kim is extremely committed to bringing the young reader
quality health education, while raising important funds for medical research. A recipient
of the National American Lung Association Presidential Award, Kim is a member of the
Authors Guild, the Publishers Marketing Association, and the Society of Children's Book
Writers and Illustrators.*

Hi, my name is Max and I'm a kid living with cancer. I have Acute Lymphatic Leukemia, or ALL, for short. Cancer happens when the cells in our bodies get all mixed up and don't do what they are supposed to. We have red blood cells and white blood cells. Red cells help us run and play. They keep us safe and help us breathe. White blood cells tell doctors how well our bodies can fight off infections, like a cold or the flu. But my white cells are building too many new cells. The new white cells are invading my red cells. It's almost like they are fighting each other!

There are lots of kids living with cancer, but not all of them have ALL.

Because my red and white blood cells are fighting, I have to get "treatments." My treatments are called chemotherapy, or chemo, for short. Chemo is a kind of medicine. Some kids with cancer get radiation treatments instead of chemotherapy. Some kids get both. My doctor says chemotherapy is like a shark that gobbles up all of my blood cells, both red and white. Chemo is very, very strong medicine. This medicine affects my whole body. My doctor told me that my hair might even fall out while I'm getting chemo treatments! There are different kinds of cancer treatments, but not everyone's hair falls out.

Please don't make fun of me if I lose my hair.

Our teacher said that if my hair does fall out, he might shave his head too. If any of you want to shave your heads, you better check with your families first!

Of course, I don't really expect you to shave your head!

Sometimes my treatments make me get a stomachache.
I might get a skin rash, or my fingernails might start looking
funny. One nurse said I might even start to like the taste of
different foods. She told me about a girl who never liked
fish. All of a sudden, the girl wanted to eat all kinds of fish!

I bet it would make my mom happy if I suddenly liked the
taste of broccoli!

Nobody knows how or why anyone gets cancer. We do know it's nobody's fault. I didn't do anything wrong to cause my cancer. You can't catch cancer from me or anybody else!

It's still okay to play with me and be my friend. I can't give you cancer.

1'm going to the hospital later today to have my first chemo treatment. They may even happen every week for a while. And the first few treatments may take a long time.

"Can we come and visit you?" my friend, Emily, in the second row wants to know.

"Sure! But no one can visit me if they are sick. I have to be especially careful about germs. That means a lot of hand washing for my family, my friends, and me," I tell her.

Our hands carry a lot of germs. Most germs you can't even see!

Yesterday I went to visit the hospital. I saw a special playroom for kids with cancer. They have lots of neat things there. There are games, movies, and even a cafeteria. I met a special nurse named Peggy who will help me and my family. She also helps my doctors and my other nurses. I will be part of a special "team." Team Max!

I met a new friend at the hospital. His name is Jeremy. He has cancer in his brain. Jeremy's cancer is different than mine. He gets radiation treatments instead of chemo. Jeremy's hair is already gone! He said it's no big deal, though. I think it looks kind of cool!!

It's nice to have a special friend when you are at the hospital.

Usually when I visit the hospital, the doctors and nurses check my blood cell counts. They want to know how many white cells and how many red cells are in my body. When all my blood cells are normal, my body is in "remission."

When I'm in remission, I feel like my old self again. I don't get tired as easily and I can do almost anything!

To give me my chemo medicine, my doctors and nurses put something called a catheter implant, or a "port," in my body. Because I use a port, I don't have to get stuck with needles! The port is put under my skin. Doctors, nurses, or my family can put my medicine in my port whenever I need it. They can do blood tests through my port too. It doesn't even hurt.

The port is much better than getting stuck with needles all the time!

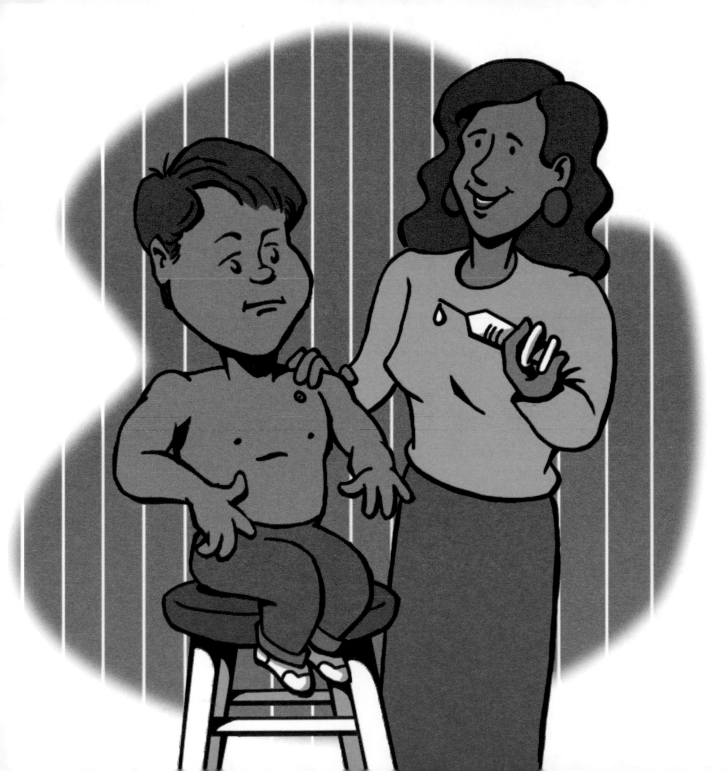

My hospital team (Team Max!) tries to figure out the best kinds of medicine and treatments for my kind of cancer. Everyone with cancer is different. My doctor thinks I will be getting treatments for about three years. It sounds like a long time, but we want to make sure to get rid of all the cancer cells in my body!

Sometimes I'll probably feel a little scared. My mom says everyone living with cancer probably feels scared. It's okay to be afraid sometimes.

Even with cancer I can still play video games and soccer. And I'm still going to try out for the baseball team! Please don't treat me any differently just because I have cancer.

After all, I'm a lot like you in every other way!

LET'S TAKE THE CANCER KIDS' QUIZ!

1. What is cancer?

Cancer happens when our cells are doing what they are not supposed to do! In ALL, white blood cells multiply too fast and invade the red blood cells. I need both happy red and white blood cells to be healthy.

2. Is every kind of cancer the same?

No. I live with ALL, but I know a boy at the hospital who has brain cancer. There are many different kinds of cancer.

3. How do children get cancer?

Scientists and doctors do not know how children get cancer. It is not something that I caused or made happen by something I did or did not do.

4. Is cancer contagious?

No, cancer is not contagious! You can't catch cancer from me or anyone else. You can still play with me and be my friend.

5. What kinds of treatments are there?

Treatments can be either chemotherapy or radiation, depending upon the cancer. Chemotherapy is a very strong medicine that will gobble up my blood cells, even my happy ones.

6. Why do we have to wash our hands so much and be careful about germs?

Because the chemotherapy will be gobbling up the cells that help my body fight off germs and infections, I will have to be very careful about germs. I should not be around any germs! You can help me by washing your hands and not playing with me if you are sick.

7. Why do you have to go to the hospital?

I will go to the hospital for treatments and other medicines. I will also go to get tests that check my body and see how it is responding to the medicine.

8. Will you miss school?

Yes, I will probably miss some school, but with your help, I do not have to miss the work. If you can help me with assignments, I can keep up with what you are learning on the days I am absent.

9. What will happen to you after you get the treatments?

It's different with each kid with cancer, but I will probably lose my hair and I might have an upset stomach. I will probably be pretty tired, but I'll still be me!

10. Will cancer change you?

I'm sure I will change a little because of the experience and the cancer, but I'll still be the same kid and you can still be my friend!

Great job! Thanks for taking the Cancer Kids' Quiz!

TEN TIPS FOR TEACHERS

✔ **1. EACH CHILD WITH CANCER IS UNIQUE.**
Each child living with cancer is unique and may respond in various ways to both the disease and the treatments. The child and his family may have different reactions, questions, and requests. Treat the child as you do all your other students, as special and unique.

✔ **2. BE PREPARED TO PROVIDE WORK OR MATERIALS FOR THE CHILD LIVING WITH CANCER.**
Many children living with cancer and their families will try to stay current with schoolwork. Many doctors recommend that the children stay in school when possible. If this is the family's plan, the student will need your help to provide materials for missed days. It may require extra effort, but your student and his family will appreciate your work.

✔ **3. WATCH FOR SIGNS THAT YOUR STUDENT'S HEALTH MAY BE DETERIORATING.**
He may be weak and tired from the treatments. Some days will be better than other days. If he is noticeably not doing well, please let the school nurse and his parents know immediately.

✔ **4. ENCOURAGE OPEN DISCUSSION IN THE CLASSROOM ABOUT WHAT IS TAKING PLACE WITH THE CHILD LIVING WITH CANCER.**
The child will likely show physical signs as a result of the treatments, possibly including loss of hair, change in skin color and nails, and changes in behavior. The child may become moody and irritable. His classmates may be concerned and need to talk in a nonthreatening, informative environment about what is happening. Allow your classroom to be a safe place to talk and encourage your students to voice concerns and fears.

✔ **5. LISTEN TO YOUR STUDENT LIVING WITH CANCER.**
Many children with cancer show exceptional bravery and are very open in talking about the disease and what they are experiencing. Be ready, however, to provide a listening ear to both the child and the family. The issues that the child and family are facing, including even possible death and deaths of children they have come to know at the hospital, can be overwhelming. Open your heart to them and be a good listener.

6. BE CONSCIENTIOUS ABOUT GERMS.

When your student with cancer is in the classroom (and even when he is not!) make sure that you and your other students are practicing safe and sanitary habits. Be sure to encourage hand washing and give careful attention to potential germs ... all the things you would normally do.

7. KEEP AN OPEN MIND.

This may be your first experience with a child living with cancer. It may require extra work on your part to get assignments to him. He may be moody and overwhelmed by the situation. Please be patient and open-minded. You will be rewarded greatly and the student and his family will be grateful.

8. COMMUNICATE WITH YOUR STUDENT'S PARENTS, CAREGIVERS, DOCTORS, AND NURSES.

The key to working with a child living with cancer and his team of helpers (including extended family) is communication. You are an essential part of that team. School is an important, stable part of the student's life. You should expect parents to tell you of any changes with the child and you should communicate the same to them.

9. TRY TO PROVIDE HELP WITH MEDICATION, IF NECESSARY.

Children living with cancer are likely to take many medications and may need friendly reminders. Talk with the school nurse. You and the student can develop a "secret code," or you can pass a note when medication is necessary.

10. TREAT THE CHILD WITH CANCER AS YOU DO ALL YOUR OTHER STUDENTS.

Just like all the children in your classroom, the child living with cancer is a unique person and wants to be recognized as one!

ADDiTiONAL RESOURCES

American Cancer Society
1599 Clifton Road NE
Atlanta, GA 32329
800-ACS-2345
www.cancer.org

**National Childhood
Cancer Foundation**
440 E. Huntington Dr.
P.O. Box 60012
Arcadia, CA 91066-6012
800-458-NCCF
www.nccf.org

Brave Kids
1592 Union Street
San Francisco, CA 94123
415-561-2393
www.bravekids.org

**The Leukemia and
Lymphoma Society**
1311 Mamaroneck Avenue
White Plains, NY 10605
914-949-5213
www.leukemia-lymphoma.org

OncoLink®
University of Pennsylvania Cancer Center
www.oncolink.upenn.edu

Band-aides & Blackboards
When Chronic Illness ... or Some Other
Medical Problem ... Goes to School
www.funrsc.fairfield.edu~jfleitas/contents.html

To order additional copies of *Taking Cancer to School* or inquire about our quantity discounts for schools, hospitals, and affiliated organizations, contact us at 1-800-999-6884.

From our *Special Kids in School*® series
Taking A.D.D. to School
Taking Asthma to School
Taking Autism to School
Taking Cerebral Palsy to School
Taking Cystic Fibrosis to School
Taking Diabetes to School
Taking Food Allergies to School
Taking Seizure Disorders to School
Taking Tourette Syndrome to School
...and others coming soon!

Other books available now!
SPORTSercise!
A School Story about
Exercise-Induced Asthma
ZooAllergy
A Fun Story about Allergy
and Asthma Triggers
Rufus Comes Home
Rufus the Bear with Diabetes™
A Story about Diagnosis and Acceptance
The ABC's of Asthma
An Asthma Alphabet Book
for Kids of All Ages
Taming the Diabetes Dragon
A Story about Living Better
with Diabetes
Trick-or-Treat for Diabetes
A Halloween Story for Kids
Living with Diabetes

From our new *Healthy Habits for Kids*™ series
There's a Louse in My House
A Fun Story about Kids and Head Lice

Coming soon ...
Playtime Is Exercise!
A Fun Story about Exercise and Play

From our new *Special Family and Friends*™ series
Allie Learns about Alzheimer's Disease
A Family Story about Love, Patience,
and Acceptance
... and others coming soon!

And from our *Substance Free Kids*® series
Smoking STINKS!!™
A Heartwarming Story about the
Importance of Avoiding Tobacco

A portion of the proceeds from all our publications is donated to various charities to help fund important medical research and education. We work hard to make a difference in the lives of children with chronic conditions and/or special needs. Thank you for your support.